Popular Music Theory

Grade Three

by

Camilla Sheldon & Tony Skinner

D1438218

A CIP record for this publication is available from the British Library.

ISBN: 1-898466-43-2

First edition © 2001 Registry Publications Ltd.

Published in Great Britain by

Registry House, Churchill Mews, Dennett Rd, Croydon, Surrey, CR0 3JH

Typesetting by

Take Note Publishing Limited, Lingfield, Surrey

Original drawings of pop performers by Chris Challinor.
Instrument photographs supplied by John Hornby Skewes Ltd.
Printed in Great Britain by MFP, Manchester.

Contents

4   **Introduction and guide to music notation**
     musical terms
     key signatures
     accidentals

6   **Scales and keys**
     major and natural minor scales
     pentatonic scales
     blues scales
     scale notes
     keys and key signatures
     blues key signatures
     scale spellings
     comparing scales

13   **Chords**
     building triads
     building chords
     chord symbols
     chord tones
     chord notation
     chord spellings
     working out chords
     comparing chords

22   **Rhythm notation**
     time signatures
     grouping of notes and rests
     distinguishing between $\frac{6}{8}$ and $\frac{3}{4}$

26   **Knowledge of popular music**
     influential performers
     instruments
     musical signs and terminology

36   **Harmony**
     technical names
     cadences
     constructing chord progressions
     improvisation

41   **Transposition**
     chord numbers
     intervals

44   **Sample answers**

47   **Examination entry form**

Introduction

This book covers all the new material you need to know to take the London College of Music Grade Three examination in Popular Music Theory.

As well as helping you to pass the examination, the intention of this book is to introduce and explain the theory behind popular music and so help you improve your musicianship. You can benefit from working through the book whether or not you intend to take an examination. You will benefit most if you try out the information you learn in this book in a practical music-making setting, by relating the information to your instrument and by using it to create your own music.

This book is part of a series that offers a structured and progressive approach to understanding the theory of popular music and whilst it can be used for independent study, it is ideally intended as a supplement to group or individual tuition.

The chapters of the book follow the sections of the examination. Each chapter outlines the facts you need to know for the examination, together with the theory behind the facts. Each chapter is completed with some examples of the types of questions that will appear in the examination paper. The sample questions are intended to provide a clear guide as to the kind of questions that may be asked in the examination, however the list of questions is neither exclusive nor exhaustive. Once you've worked through the questions at the end of each section, you can check your answers by looking at the 'sample answers' in the back of the book.

As the requirements for each examination are cumulative, it is essential that you have a knowledge of the requirements for the previous grades. If you are not already familiar with this earlier material, it is recommended that you study the preceding handbooks in this series.

Examinations are held twice a year and you can only enter for an examination by completing the stamped entry form at the back of each handbook.

We hope you enjoy working through this book and wish you success with the examination and all your musical endeavours.

Camilla Sheldon and Tony Skinner

In the examination, you can use either the treble clef (G clef) or the bass clef (F clef) to write your answers. The basics of reading and writing music notation are covered in the earlier books in this series. Below are a few 'reminder notes'.

musical terms

Sometimes there are two different names that can be used for the same musical element. Also, the terminology that is widely used in N. America (and increasingly amongst pop, rock and jazz musicians in the U.K. and elsewhere) is different to that traditionally used in the U.K. and other parts of Europe.

A summary of the main alternative terms is shown below. In the examination you can use either version. In this book we generally use the terms shown in the left-hand column, as these are the ones that are more commonly used amongst popular music musicians.

whole note	=	semibreve
half note	=	minim
quarter note	=	crotchet
eighth note	=	quaver
sixteenth note	=	semiquaver
whole step	=	whole tone
half step	=	semitone
staff	=	stave
treble clef	=	G clef
bass clef	=	F clef
measures	=	bars
keynote	=	tonic
$\frac{4}{4}$	=	**C**
flag	=	tail
leger line	=	ledger line
flattened 3rd, 6th or 7th	=	minor 3rd, 6th or 7th
flattened 5th	=	diminished 5th

key signatures

Key signatures are written at the start of every staff, and each key signature is always written in the same way, as shown below:

- When you write an F# in a key signature always write it across the F line.

- When you write a C# in a key signature always write it in the C space.

- When you write a B♭ in a key signature always write it across the B line.

- When you write an E♭ in a key signature always write it in the E space.

accidentals

When a flat, sharp or natural sign is written before a note during a piece of music it is called an *accidental*.

A *natural* (♮) sign means that the note is returned to its 'natural' version. For example: C# would become C, E♭ would become E.

Section One – scales and keys

In this section of the exam you will be asked to write out and identify some of the following scales (and their key signatures):

Scales with key signatures to the range of two sharps and two flats:

- major
- pentatonic major
- minor
- pentatonic minor
- blues scales: C, G, D, F and B♭.

The scales that have been added for the Grade Three exam are:

- B♭ major
- B♭ pentatonic major
- G natural minor
- G pentatonic minor
- C, G, D, F and B♭ blues scales

In this book we only cover in detail these additional Grade Three scales, so if you are unsure about any of the other scale requirements you should study the previous books in this series.

So that the scales learnt in theory can be used effectively in a practical way, you should be able to do the following:

- Write out, and identify, the *letter names* that make up each scale.

- Write out, and identify, each scale in standard *music notation* (adding or identifying the key signature where appropriate). You can write your answers in either the treble clef or the bass clef.

- Write out, and identify, the *scale spelling* of each scale.

the theory

major & natural minor scales

Major scales and *natural minor scales* are constructed using a combination of *whole steps* (*whole tones*) and *half steps* (*semitones*).

<u>Major scales</u> are constructed using the pattern of whole steps and half steps shown below:

W   W   H   W   W   W   H

Here is the B♭ major scale as an example.

notes: B♭ C D E♭ F G A B♭
pattern: W   W   H   W   W   W   H

If you memorise the major scale 'step-pattern' (W W H W W W H) you will always be able to find out which notes make up any of the major scales. Simply start with the keynote and then use the step-pattern to find the other notes – making sure that, apart from the repetition of the keynote at the octave, each letter name is used only once. This will ensure that the correct 'enharmonic spelling' will be used for each scale.

<u>Natural minor scales</u> are constructed using this step-pattern:

W   H   W   W   H   W   W

(Note that this is the same step-pattern as if the major scale is started on its sixth degree).

Here is the G natural minor scale as an example.

notes: **G A Bb C D Eb F G**
pattern: **W H W W H W W**

Notice how the pattern of whole and half steps used to create the G natural minor scale results in Bb and Eb notes being used.

If you memorise the natural minor scale 'step-pattern' (W H W W H W W) you will always be able to find out which notes make up any of the natural minor scales. Simply start with the keynote and then use the step-pattern to find the other notes – making sure that, apart from the repetition of the keynote at the octave, each letter name is used only once.

pentatonic scales

The pentatonic major and pentatonic minor are both five-note scales.

<u>Pentatonic major scales</u> are made up of five notes taken from the major scale with the same keynote. The five notes are the 1st, 2nd, 3rd, 5th and 6th. Notice that it is the 4th and 7th notes of the major scale that are omitted to create a pentatonic major scale. The notes in the Bb pentatonic major scale are therefore Bb, C, D, F and G. (When played or written as a scale the octave is also included.)

<u>Pentatonic minor scales</u> are made up of five notes (the 1st, 3rd, 4th, 5th and 7th) taken from the natural minor scale with the same keynote. Notice that it is the 2nd and 6th notes of the natural minor scale that are omitted to create a pentatonic minor scale. The notes in the G pentatonic minor are therefore G, Bb, C, D and F. (When played or written as a scale the octave is also included.)

blues scales

The *blues scale* is a six-note scale. It uses notes from the major scale, but lowers some of them by a half step. The notes taken from the major scale are the 1st, 3rd, 4th, 5th and 7th, however the 3rd, 5th and 7th notes are all lowered by one half step to create the *blue notes*. The b3rd and b7th notes replace the 3rd and 7th notes of the major scale, but the b5th note is used *in addition to* the 5th note of the major scale. The blues scale therefore contains the 1st, b3rd, 4th, b5th, 5th and b7th. For example, the notes in the C blues scale are C, Eb, F, Gb, G and Bb. (When played or written as a scale the octave is also included.)

---

b5 / #4

The b5 note within the blues scale is sometimes referred to as a #4. For example, in the C blues scale, Gb may be called F# by some musicians. This is because in music notation it is traditionally 'correct' to avoid writing two notes on the 5th degree of the scale, hence the #4 note is used instead. However, blues does not readily conform to the traditions of standard music notation and the term b5 is now commonly used (and notated) in the blues scale amongst blues, jazz and rock musicians. For this reason, whenever referring to the blues scale in this book, the term b5 will be used and the notes and scale numbers will be named accordingly. In the exam, you can use either term – b5 or #4 – with the appropriate note names and scale numbers, but you must be consistent in your use.

---

scale notes

Here are the names of the notes contained within the additional scales that are required for the Grade Three exam.

Bb major:	Bb	C	D	Eb	F	G	A	Bb
Bb pentatonic major:		Bb	C	D	F	G	Bb
G natural minor:	G	A	Bb	C	D	Eb	F	G
G pentatonic minor:		G	Bb	C	D	F	G
C blues:		C	Eb	F	Gb	G	Bb	C
G blues:		G	Bb	C	Db	D	F	G
D blues:		D	F	G	Ab	A	C	D
F blues:		F	Ab	Bb	Cb	C	Eb	F
Bb blues:		Bb	Db	Eb	Fb	F	Ab	Bb

You should try and play these scales on your instrument so that you can hear the sound of them. It will also help you to memorise the notes that make up each scale. If you forget the names of the notes in these scales, you can work them out in the following ways:

1. For major and natural minor scales: use the 'step-pattern' to work out the notes of the scale. Be careful to ensure that, apart from the repetition of the keynote at the octave, *each letter name is used only once*. This rule applies to all scales at this grade (apart from the fifth degrees of the blues scale) and ensures that the correct *enharmonic spelling* is used for each scale. For example, in the B♭ major scale notice how a half step above D becomes E♭, rather than D#.

2. For pentatonic major and minor scales: use the procedure described above to work out the appropriate major or natural minor scale and then select the five notes that you need for the pentatonic scale you require.

3. For blues scales: work out the major scale, with the same starting note, using the 'step-pattern', and then select the six notes you need for the blues scale – lowering the appropriate notes by a half step. Remember you need to include the ♭5th *and* the ♮5th notes.

Remember that for every scale (apart from the fifth degrees of the blues scale) each letter name should be used only once (apart from the repetition of the keynote at the octave).

keys and key signatures

Each key signature represents both a major key and its *relative minor* key.

■ Two sharps – F# and C#, is the key signature for both D major and B minor.

■ One sharp – F#, is the key signature for both G major and E minor.

■ Two flats – B♭ and E♭, is the key signature for both B♭ major and G minor.

■ One flat – B♭, is the key signature for both F major and D minor.

■ No sharps or flats is the key signature for both C major and A minor.

You can usually identify whether the key of a piece of music is major or minor by its overall sound; sometimes you can also identify this by seeing which note the melody begins or ends with. If a piece of music has two flats in the key signature and begins and ends on the note of B♭, then it is likely to be in the key of B♭ major; if the melody begins and ends on the note of G it is likely to be in the key of G minor. If the chords are shown, then you can normally identify the key from the first and last chord.

In music notation, key signatures are written after the clef and before the time signature at the start of the music, and are repeated on every staff.

Here are the key signatures and scale notation for the major, pentatonic major, natural minor and pentatonic minor scales that have been added for the Grade Three exam.

B♭ major

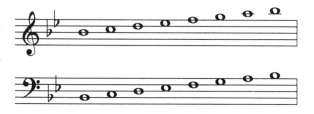

B♭ pentatonic major

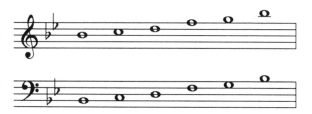

G natural minor

G pentatonic minor.

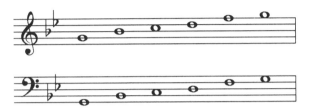

blues key signatures

Blues music does not fit neatly into the traditional rules of music theory that were originally developed for classical music. Because blues scales have a minor third interval between the 1st and 3rd notes of the scale, it might appear that they should use minor key signatures. However, it is generally considered that major key signatures are more appropriate for blues. The reason for this is that blues music is normally based on 'dominant harmony' – in other words, the chordal accompaniment to a blues usually consists of dominant 7th chords. As dominant 7th chords are essentially 'major' chords, this creates an underlying 'major harmony' which is best reflected by the use of major key signatures. The fact that the melody or improvisation uses *flattened* notes against these major chords is simply a reflection of the method that blues music uses to create the musical tensions which form the core of the 'blues' sound.

Although using major key signatures means that a number of accidentals will have to be used when notating music taken from the blues scale, this is actually an advantage as it immediately demonstrates to the reader that the written music is blues-based and not in a standard major or minor key.

The key signature for each blues scale is therefore the same as for the major scale of the same starting pitch:

The D blues scale has a key signature of two sharps – F# and C#

The G blues scale has a key signature of one sharp – F#

The Bb blues scale has a key signature of two flats – Bb and Eb

The F blues scale has a key signature of one flat – Bb

The C blues scale has a key signature of no sharps or flats.

Remember that the above is a combination of two musical traditions and reflects the most common current usage. For blues scales and keys, the key signature only tells you what the key centre is – it does NOT tell you which notes are in the scale. In fact, each blues scale will need to use several accidentals as a result of the key signature.

C blues

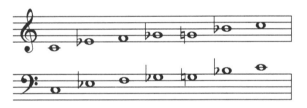

G blues

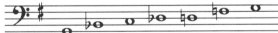

D blues

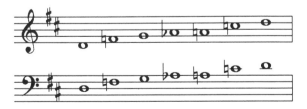

F blues

B♭ blues

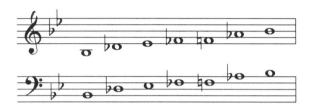

enharmonic spellings

The F♭ note in the B♭ blues scale is another way of describing the pitch 'E'; just as the C♭ in the F blues scale is the same pitch as 'B'. Whilst there would be no difference in the sound of either version, it is important in all scales that the pitch name of the note matches the corresponding scale degree. For example, in G blues scale, the minor third is notated as B♭ (rather than A#) because the letter B is a 3rd higher than G (whereas the letter A is only a 2nd higher).

scale spellings

In popular music, instead of using the letter names of the notes in a scale, musicians often use numbers. This is called the *scale spelling*. Each note of the scale is given a number, starting with the keynote as '1'. For example, in B♭ major the notes would be numbered as follows:

B♭ C D E♭ F G A B♭
1 2 3 4 5 6 7 8

The numbers refer to the *intervals* between the keynote and each other note in the scale. For example, rather than talking about the F note in the scale of B♭ major, pop musicians might refer to it as the 5th of B♭.

Each type of scale has a unique scale spelling and this enables easy comparison between different scale types.

Major scales are numbered like this:

1 2 3 4 5 6 7 8

All other scales are numbered in comparison to the major scale.

Natural minor scales are numbered like this:

1 2 ♭3 4 5 ♭6 ♭7 8

Below is an explanation as to why the natural minor scale is numbered this way. In the examination you will only be asked to identify, or write out the scale spelling.

Supplementary explanation

The appearance of a ♭ sign in a scale spelling does not mean that the note which occurs on that scale degree is necessarily a flat note. Instead, the flat sign is used, in this instance, as a method of indicating that this scale degree creates a 'minor' (i.e. smaller) interval when compared to the major scale – i.e. the distance between the keynote and this scale degree is a half step smaller than the distance between the keynote and the corresponding scale degree in the major scale with the same starting note. For example, the interval between G and B♭ (the third degree of the G natural minor scale) is a half step smaller than the interval between G and B (the third degree of the G major scale). In fact, the 3rd, 6th and 7th degrees of the natural minor scale are all 'minor' intervals when compared to the major scale. (You can work this out for yourself by counting the number of half steps between the keynotes and these degrees of the scales). Although the meaning is exactly the same, pop musicians generally prefer to call these intervals 'flattened' (rather than minor), and consequently a ♭ is placed before them to indicate this. An example is given below, showing the comparison between the two scale types and the consequent difference in the scale spelling.

G major scale
G A B C D E F# G
1 2 3 4 5 6 7   8

G natural minor scale
G A B♭ C D E♭ F G
1 2 ♭3 4 5 ♭6 ♭7 8

Pentatonic major scales are numbered like this:

| 1 2 3 5 6 8 |

The scale spelling of the pentatonic major scale is based on that of the major scale, but because the pentatonic major scale does not include the 4th or 7th notes of the major scale, these scale numbers are omitted.

Pentatonic minor scales are numbered like this:

| 1 ♭3 4 5 ♭7 8 |

The scale spelling of the pentatonic minor scale is based on the natural minor scale, but because the pentatonic minor scale does not include the 2nd or ♭6th notes of the natural minor scale these scale numbers are omitted.

Blues scales are numbered like this:

| 1 ♭3 4 ♭5 5 ♭7 8 |

Below you will find a brief explanation as to why the blues scale is numbered this way. In the exam, however, you will only be asked to identify, or write out the scale spelling.

Supplementary explanation

The scale spelling of the blues scale is numbered in comparison to the major scale. The blues scale contains the 4th and 5th notes of the major scale, but not the 2nd or 6th notes so these scale numbers are omitted. The 3rd and 7th notes are *flattened* in comparison to the major scale, as the intervals between the keynote and these scale degrees are a half step smaller than the intervals between the keynote and the same scale degrees in the major scale.

The additional note – the ♭5th – is called a *flattened* or *diminished* interval. This is because it is one half step nearer to the keynote than the (perfect) 5th note that is also contained in the scale.

The full name for the interval between the 1st and 5th degrees in all the scales covered so far (including the blues scale) is a *perfect fifth*. Unlike the other intervals we have looked at, when perfect 5th intervals are made smaller by one half step they are not called 'minor' intervals, instead they are known as *flattened* (or *diminished*) 5th *intervals*.

comparing scales

You can use your knowledge of major scales and scale spellings to work out the notes contained in all other scales. For example, by knowing which notes are contained in the G major scale it is possible to work out which notes are contained in the G pentatonic major, G natural minor, G pentatonic minor and G blues scales.

major scale:	1	2	3	4	5	6	7	8
G major:	G	A	B	C	D	E	F#	G
pentatonic major:	1	2	3		5	6		8
G pentatonic major:	G	A	B		D	E		G
natural minor:	1	2	♭3	4	5	♭6	♭7	8
G natural minor:	G	A	B♭	C	D	E♭	F	G
pentatonic minor:	1		♭3	4	5		♭7	8
G pentatonic minor:	G		B♭	C	D		F	G
blues:	1	♭3	4	♭5	5	♭7	8	
G blues:	G	B♭	C	D♭	D	F	G	

Alternatively, scales can also be compared directly with each other (without reference to the major scale). For example:

- the pentatonic minor scale is the same as the natural minor scale with the 2nd and 6th notes omitted;

- the blues scale, except for the addition of the ♭5th note, is exactly the same as the pentatonic minor scale.

the exam

Below are some examples of the types of questions that candidates may be asked in this section of the exam. If you can't answer a question, then carefully re-read the preceding chapter and, if necessary, refer to the preceding books in this series.

When answering questions that involve writing scales in notation, you can write them in either the treble or bass clef. Either way, you need only write them ascending using whole notes.

Q1. Use letter names to write out the notes of the D blues scale.

A1. _____

Q2. Use letter names to write out the notes of the natural minor scale that has two flats in the key signature.

A2. _____

Q3. Write out the scale spelling of the blues scale.

A3. _____

Q4. Using the correct key signature and appropriate accidentals, write one octave of the B♭ blues scale in either the treble or bass clef.

A4. _____
_____
_____
_____
_____

Q5. Using the correct key signature, write one octave of the B♭ major scale in either the treble or bass clef.

A5. _____
_____
_____
_____
_____

Section Two – chords

In this section of the exam you will be asked to write out and identify some of the following chords:

- All major, minor and diminished triads from major and natural minor scales within a range of keys to 2 sharps and 2 flats.

- C major 7th, G major 7th, D major 7th, F major 7th, B♭ major 7th

- A minor 7th, E minor 7th, B minor 7th, D minor 7th, G minor 7th

- G dominant 7th, D dominant 7th, A dominant 7th, C dominant 7th
  F dominant 7th

So that the chords learnt in theory can be used effectively in a practical way, you should be able to do the following:

- Use *chord symbols* to identify the chords.

- Write out, and identify, the *letter names* that make up each chord.

- Write out, and identify, each chord in standard *music notation*. You can write your answers in either the treble clef or the bass clef.

- Write out, and identify, the *chord spelling* of each chord and name the *intervals* between the root and each chord tone.

the theory

building triads

All the triads at this grade are built by taking alternate notes from a scale. For example, major triads can be built by starting with the first note of the major scale, then omitting the 2nd note of the scale and taking the 3rd, and then omitting the 4th note and taking the 5th. So, the B♭ major triad, for instance, contains the first, third and fifth notes of the B♭ major scale.

B♭ major scale	B♭ major triad
B♭ C D E♭ F G A B♭	B♭ D F

Each triad is made up of a root (the first note), a third and a fifth. As well as being built on the first degree of a scale, triads can be built starting on all the degrees of a scale. Each degree of the scale becomes the root

for its related triad, and the triads are built by taking three alternate notes of the scale.

The additional type of triad that is introduced at Grade Three is the *diminished triad*. This is created by building a triad starting from the seventh degree of a major scale. For example:

C major scale	B diminished triad
C D E F G A B	B D F
B♭ major scale	A diminished triad
B♭ C D E♭ F G A	A C E♭

This triad can also be built by starting on the second note of a natural minor scale.

Here is the C major scale with all the triads that can be built on each degree of the scale.

C major scale	triad	degree	chord tones
<u>C</u> D <u>E</u> F <u>G</u> A B	C	I	C E G
C <u>D</u> E <u>F</u> G <u>A</u> B	Dm	II	D F A
C D <u>E</u> F <u>G</u> A <u>B</u>	Em	III	E G B
<u>C</u> D E <u>F</u> G <u>A</u> B	F	IV	F A C
C <u>D</u> E F <u>G</u> A <u>B</u>	G	V	G B D
<u>C</u> D <u>E</u> F G <u>A</u> B	Am	VI	A C E
C <u>D</u> E <u>F</u> G A <u>B</u>	B°	VII	B D F

Notice that the triads on the 1st, 4th and 5th degrees are major, the triads on the 2nd, 3rd and 6th degrees are minor, and the triad on the 7th degree is diminished. All major keys have this – major, minor, minor, major, major, minor, diminished – pattern of triads.

Below are all the triads as they occur in the keys of C, G, D, F and B♭ major.

scale/degree:	I	II	III	IV	V	VI	VII
C major:	C	Dm	Em	F	G	Am	B°
G major:	G	Am	Bm	C	D	Em	F#°
D major:	D	Em	F#m	G	A	Bm	C#°
F major:	F	Gm	Am	B♭	C	Dm	E°
B♭ major:	B♭	Cm	Dm	E♭	F	Gm	A°

Here is the A natural minor scale, with the triads that can be built on each degree of the scale.

A natural minor scale	triad	degree	chord tones
<u>A</u> B <u>C</u> D <u>E</u> F G	Am	I	A C E
A <u>B</u> C <u>D</u> E <u>F</u> G	B°	II	B D F
A B <u>C</u> D <u>E</u> F <u>G</u>	C	III	C E G
A B C <u>D</u> E <u>F</u> G	Dm	IV	D F A
A <u>B</u> C D <u>E</u> F <u>G</u>	Em	V	E G B
A B <u>C</u> D E <u>F</u> G	F	VI	F A C
A <u>B</u> C <u>D</u> E F <u>G</u>	G	VII	G B D

Notice that the triads on the 1st, 4th and 5th degrees are minor, the triads on the 3rd, 6th and 7th degrees are major and the triad on the 2nd degree is diminished. All natural minor keys have this – minor, diminished, major, minor, minor, major, major – pattern of triads.

Below are the triads built from the scales of A, E, B, D and G natural minor.

scale/degree:	I	II	III	IV	V	VI	VII
A minor:	Am	B°	C	Dm	Em	F	G
E minor:	Em	F#°	G	Am	Bm	C	D
B minor:	Bm	C#°	D	Em	F#m	G	A
D minor:	Dm	E°	F	Gm	Am	B♭	C
G minor:	Gm	A°	B♭	Cm	Dm	E♭	F

building chords

In the same way that triads are built by taking three alternate notes from a scale, major 7th, minor 7th and dominant 7th chords are built by taking four alternate notes from a scale. For example, the B♭ major 7th chord contains the first, third, fifth and seventh notes of the B♭ major scale.

B♭ major scale	B♭ major 7th chord
<u>B♭</u> C <u>D</u> E♭ <u>F</u> G <u>A</u> B♭	B♭ D F A

Major 7th, minor 7th and dominant 7th chords are all made up of a root (the first note), a third, a fifth and a seventh. By starting on specific degrees of the major scale, major 7th, minor 7th and dominant 7th chords can be built by taking four alternate notes from the scale. At this grade, however, you are only required to know the chords that are built on the first and fifth degrees of a major scale and the first degree of the natural minor scale.

- The chord that is built on the first degree of the major scale, by taking four alternate notes, is always a major seventh chord.

- The chord that is built on the first degree of a natural minor scale, by taking four alternate notes, is always a minor 7th chord.

- The chord that is built on the fifth degree of the major scale, by taking four alternate notes, is always a dominant 7th chord.

For example:

The chord that is built on the fifth degree of the B♭ major scale is the F dominant 7th chord.

B♭ major scale	F dominant 7th chord
B♭ <u>C</u> D E♭ <u>F</u> G <u>A</u> B♭	F A C E♭

The chord that is built on the fifth degree of the D major scale is the A dominant 7th chord.

D major scale	A dominant 7th chord
D <u>E</u> F# <u>G</u> A B <u>C</u># D	A C# E G

chord symbols

■ The symbol for a *major triad* is the capital letter of the chord; so the symbol for the B♭ major triad is *B♭*.

(Although some musicians add 'maj', or 'ma', after the letter name this is not recommended; it is unnecessary to add any suffix to the major chord symbol.)

■ The symbol for a *minor triad* is the capital letter of the chord, plus a lower case 'm'; so the symbol for the G minor triad is *Gm*.

(Some musicians add 'min' or 'mi' after the letter name for extra clarity – which is acceptable. Other methods of writing the minor chord symbol, such as 'G-', are best avoided.)

■ The symbol for a *diminished triad* is the capital letter of the chord plus °; so the chord symbol for the B diminished triad is *B°*.

(If preferred, diminished triads can also be written like this: *Bdim*.)

■ The symbol for a *major 7th* chord is the capital letter of the chord, plus 'maj7'; so the symbol for the B♭ major 7th chord is *B♭maj7*.

(Major 7th chords are sometimes also written like this: B♭M7, B♭ma7, B♭△ or B♭△7. Although all these methods are in current usage, the suffix 'maj7' is preferable, as this is the clearest and most commonly used symbol for a major 7th chord.)

■ The symbol for a *minor 7th* chord is the capital letter plus 'm7'; so the symbol for the G minor 7th chord is *Gm7*.

(Some musicians add 'min7' or 'mi7' after the letter name for extra clarity – which is acceptable. Other methods of writing the minor chord symbol, such as 'G-7', are best avoided.)

■ The symbol for a *dominant 7th* chord is the capital letter plus '7'; so the chord symbol for the F dominant 7th chord is *F7*.

chord tones

Below are the triads that have been added for the Grade Three exam, listed with their chord tones. Together with the triads covered in the previous grades, these make up all the triads that are built (by taking three alternate notes) from the C, G, D, F and B♭ major scales.

major triads			
A:	A	C#	E
B♭:	B♭	D	F
E♭:	E♭	G	B♭

minor triads			
F#m:	F#	A	C#
Gm:	G	B♭	D
Cm:	C	E♭	G

diminished triads			
B°:	B	D	F
F#°:	F#	A	C
C#°:	C#	E	G
E°:	E	G	B♭
A°:	A	C	E♭

Here are the 7th chords that have been added for the Grade Three exam. All the other 7th chords required for the grade have been covered in previous books in this series.

seventh chords				
B♭maj7:	B♭	D	F	A
Gm7:	G	B♭	D	F
F7:	F	A	C	E♭

chord notation

Here are the chords that have been added for the Grade Three exam, written out in both the treble clef and the bass clef:

A

B♭

E♭

F#m

Gm

Cm

B°

F#°

C#°

E°

A°

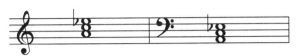

B♭maj7

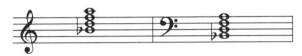

Gm7

F7

chord spellings

In the same way that pop musicians often use numbers to talk about the notes in a scale, they also use numbers to talk about the notes in a chord. This is called the *chord spelling*. Each note in the chord is given a number, which refers to the *interval* between that note and the root of the chord.

Each type of chord has a unique chord spelling. This enables easy comparison between different chord types.

For example:

B♭ major triad is numbered like this:

B♭	D	F
1	3	5

B♭ major 7th is numbered like this:

B♭	D	F	A
1	3	5	7

In both these examples, rather than talking about the F note in the chord, pop musicians might refer to it as the *5th* of the chord.

In a major chord or scale, the interval between the root and third is called a *major third*, the interval between the root and the fifth is properly known as a *perfect fifth*, and the interval between the root and the seventh is called a *major seventh*.

This means that major triads and major 7th chords have a *major third* interval between the root and the 3rd note, and a *perfect fifth* interval between the root and the fifth note. A major 7th chord also has a *major seventh* interval between the root and the 7th note.

Major triads are numbered like this:

1 3 5

This is because the intervals between the root and the third note, and the root and the fifth note, in a major triad are the same as the intervals between the keynote and the third and fifth notes of the major scale.

Major 7th chords are numbered like this:

1 3 5 7

This is because the intervals between the root and third, fifth and seventh notes in a major 7th chord are exactly the same as between the keynote and the third, fifth and seventh notes of the major scale.

All other chord types are numbered in comparison to the major 7th chord (or major scale).

Minor triads are numbered like this:

1 ♭3 5

Minor 7th chords are numbered like this:

1 ♭3 5 ♭7

Notice that minor triads, and minor 7th chords, have a *flattened* (i.e. *minor*) *third* interval, and a *perfect fifth* interval. Minor 7th chords also have a *flattened* (i.e. *minor*) *seventh* interval.

Dominant 7th chords are numbered like this:

1 3 5 ♭7

Notice that the dominant 7th chord has a *major third* interval, a *perfect fifth* interval, and a *flattened* (i.e. *minor*) *seventh* interval.

Diminished triads are numbered like this:

1 ♭3 ♭5

Notice that diminished triads have a *flattened* (i.e. *minor*) *third* interval. Also, the interval between the root and the fifth is one half step smaller than the corresponding interval in a major or minor triad. This type of interval is known as a *flattened fifth* (or *diminished fifth*) interval.

Note that an interval that is one half step smaller than a *major* interval is known as a *flattened* (or 'minor') interval, whereas an interval that is one half step smaller than a *perfect* interval is known as a *flattened* (or 'diminished') interval.

There follows a brief explanation as to why the minor triad, minor 7th chord, dominant 7th chord and diminished triad are numbered as they are. In the examination, however, you will only be asked to identify, or write out the chord spelling, and give the names of the intervals between the root and the chord tones of the chord types listed.

Supplementary explanation

Any chord which contains a *flattened* (i.e. *minor* or *diminished*) interval has a flat sign before the number in the chord spelling. This is because the interval is one half step (semitone) smaller than the corresponding interval in a major chord or scale.

For example, between D and F# (root and 3rd in Dmaj7) there are four half steps, whilst between D and F (root and 3rd in Dm7) there are only three half steps. Consequently, the third in a minor, diminished or minor 7th chord is called a flattened 3rd (♭3), or minor 3rd. For similar reasons, the seventh in a dominant 7th or minor 7th chord is a called a flattened 7th (♭7) or minor 7th, and the fifth in a diminished triad is called a flattened 5th (♭5) or diminished 5th.

working out chords

All the chords in this section are derived from the major and natural minor scales in Section One. Many of the major and minor triads are built on the keynote of one of the major or natural minor scales, however some of the major and minor triads and all of the diminished triads and dominant 7th chords are built on degrees of the scale other than the first degree. There are several methods by which you can work out the notes in any of the Grade Three chords, but the most straightforward method for each chord type is outlined below:

1. Major triads occur on the 1st, 4th and 5th degrees of the major scale. Therefore, by identifying the major scale in which the root note of the triad occurs on one of these degrees, and then taking three alternate notes (the 1st, 3rd and 5th) starting from this degree of the scale, you can work out the notes in the triad.

   For example: Eb is the 4th note in the scale of Bb major. So by taking three alternate notes starting from this degree of the Bb scale you will discover the notes in the Eb major triad (Eb, G and Bb).

2. Minor triads occur on the 2nd, 3rd and 6th degrees of the major scale. Therefore, by identifying the major scale in which the root note of the triad occurs on one of these degrees, and then taking three alternate notes (the 1st, 3rd and 5th) starting from this degree of the scale, you can work out the notes in the triad.

   For example: C is the 2nd note in the scale of Bb major. So by taking three alternate notes starting from the 2nd degree of the Bb scale you will discover the notes in the C minor triad (C, Eb and G).

3. Diminished triads occur on the 7th degree of the major scale. Therefore, by identifying the major scale in which the root note of the triad occurs on the 7th degree, and then taking three alternate notes (the 1st, 3rd and 5th) starting from this degree of the scale, you can work out the notes in the diminished triad.

   For example: A is the 7th note in the scale of Bb major. So by taking three alternate notes starting from the 7th degree of the Bb scale you will discover the notes in the A diminished triad (A, C and Eb).

4. Dominant 7th chords occur on the 5th degree of the major scale. Therefore, by identifying the major scale in which the root note of the chord occurs on the 5th degree, and then taking four alternate notes (the 1st, 3rd, 5th and 7th) starting from this degree of the scale, you can work out the notes in the dominant 7th chord.

   For example: F is the 5th note in the scale of Bb major. So by taking four alternate notes starting from the 5th degree of the Bb scale you will discover the notes in the F dominant 7th chord (F, A, C and Eb).

5. Major seventh chords can be worked out by simply taking the 1st, 3rd, 5th and 7th notes of the major scale with the same starting note.

   For example: by taking the 1st, 3rd, 5th and 7th notes of the Bb major scale you will discover the notes in the Bb major 7th chord (Bb, D, F and A).

6. Minor seventh chords can be worked by relating them to major scales, but an easier method is simply to take the 1st, 3rd, 5th and 7th notes of the natural minor scale with the same starting note.

   For example: by taking the 1st, 3rd, 5th and 7th notes of the G natural minor scale you will discover the notes in the G minor 7th chord (G, Bb, D and F).

For all the above, it is essential that the notes of the scales are identified correctly – in particular, ensure that you take account of any sharps or flats that arise in the key.

comparing chords

You can use your knowledge of major chords and chord spellings to work out the notes contained in all other chords. For example, by knowing which notes are contained in the D major triad and Dmaj7 chord it is possible to work out which notes are contained in the D minor triad, D diminished triad, Dmin7 and D7 chords:

major triad: D:	1 D	3 F#	5 A	
minor triad: Dm:	1 D	♭3 F	5 A	
diminished triad: D°:	1 D	♭3 F	♭5 A♭	
major 7th chord: Dmaj7:	1 D	3 F#	5 A	7 C#
minor 7th chord: Dm7:	1 D	♭3 F	5 A	♭7 C
dom 7th chord : D7:	1 D	3 F#	5 A	♭7 C

Alternatively, chords can also be compared directly with each other (without reference to the major 7th chord). For example:

- a diminished triad only differs from a minor triad in that the fifth is a flattened, not a perfect, fifth interval from the root.

- a minor 7th chord only differs from a dominant 7th in that the third is a minor, not a major, third interval from the root.

- a dominant 7th chord only differs from a major 7th chord in that the seventh is a flattened, not a major, 7th interval from the root.

the exam

Below are some examples of the types of questions that candidates may be asked in this section of the exam. If you can't answer a question, then carefully re-read the preceding chapter and, if necessary, refer to the previous books in this series.

When answering questions that involve writing chords in notation, you can write your answers in either the treble clef or the bass clef. You should place the notes of each chord vertically on top of one another, using whole notes. The notes of each chord should be written in *root position*, that means put the root note at the bottom, then write the third note, then the fifth and finally (where appropriate) the seventh.

Q1. Write the notes of the F7 chord using letter names.

A1. _____

Q2. Which type of chord has the following chord spelling? 1 ♭3 5 ♭7

A2. _____

Q3. Write out the *chord spelling* for the major 7th chord.

A3. _____

Q4. What is the name of the type of interval between the notes of E and B♭ in an E diminished triad?

A4. _____

Q5. Write out the A7 chord in either the treble or bass clef.

A5. _____

Section Three – rhythm notation

In this section of the exam you will be asked to use some of the following note and rest values in $\frac{4}{4}$ $\frac{3}{4}$ $\frac{2}{4}$ or $\frac{6}{8}$ time:

- whole notes (semibreves)
- half notes (minims)
- quarter notes (crotchets)
- eighth notes (quavers)
- sixteenth notes (semiquavers)

- whole rests (semibreve rests)
- half rests (minim rests)
- quarter rests (crotchet rests)
- eighth rests (quaver rests)
- sixteenth rests (semiquaver rests)

- dotted notes and rests (for all of the above, where appropriate, except for sixteenth notes).

So that the rhythm notation learnt in theory can be used effectively in a practical way, you should be able to do the following:

- Explain how notes and rests of different value fit into bars (measures) of $\frac{4}{4}$ $\frac{3}{4}$ $\frac{2}{4}$ or $\frac{6}{8}$ time.

- Group notes and rests correctly within $\frac{4}{4}$ $\frac{3}{4}$ $\frac{2}{4}$ or $\frac{6}{8}$ time.

- Compose simple rhythms in $\frac{4}{4}$ $\frac{3}{4}$ $\frac{2}{4}$ or $\frac{6}{8}$ time, using the note and rest values listed above.

the theory

The basics of rhythm notation are covered in the earlier books in this series and you should refer to them if you are unsure of any of the terms and concepts mentioned below.

time signatures

$\frac{4}{4}$ time means that there are four quarter note (crotchet) beats in every bar.

$\frac{3}{4}$ time means that there are three quarter note (crotchet) beats in every bar.

$\frac{2}{4}$ time means that there are two quarter note (crotchet) beats in every bar.

$\frac{2}{4}$, $\frac{3}{4}$ and $\frac{4}{4}$ are all known as *simple time*. In these time signatures each beat is represented by a quarter note which can be divided into two. For example, in $\frac{3}{4}$ time any of the three beats can be divided in two as follows:

$\frac{6}{8}$ is a *compound* time signature; although in $\frac{6}{8}$ time there is an equivalent of six eighth notes in a bar, there are only two main beats – two dotted quarter notes, each comprising three eighth notes pulses. So in $\frac{6}{8}$ time, each of its two beats can be divided into three:

Notice that in simple time signatures the upper figure represents the number of beats per bar, whereas in $\frac{6}{8}$ time the upper number represents the number of pulses (which is three times the number of beats in the bar).

grouping of notes and rests

There are certain rules about how notes and rests can be grouped. These exist in music notation so that all the beats of the bar can be clearly identified, and consequently the written music is easier to read.

At this level you should be aware of the following rules and the exceptions to these rules.

simple time signatures

<u>RULE 1</u>

Quarter notes, and notes shorter than a quarter note, are beamed together when they belong to one beat.

For example:

Exceptions

i) In a bar of 4/4 time, you can beam together all eighth and sixteenth notes that are in the first half of a bar (beats one and two) or in the second half of the bar (beats three and four). However, you should not beam together notes across the middle of the bar (beats two and three).

ii) In 2/4 and 3/4 time you can beam together all eighth and sixteenth notes within a bar.

For example:

<u>RULE 2</u>

When you write rests, each beat and each half beat must be completed with the appropriate rests. This is because it is much easier to read music if you can clearly see where each beat and each half beat starts.

For example:

<u>Exceptions</u>

i) In a bar of 4/4 time you can write a half (minim) rest in the first half of the bar (beats one and two) or in the second half of the bar (beats three and four). However, you should not write a half rest in the middle of the bar (beats two and three) – instead you should use two quarter (crotchet) rests.

ii) The whole note (semibreve) rest (also known as the 'whole bar' rest), indicates a whole bar rest in all popular time signatures, including 2/4 and 3/4. Consequently, dotted half note rests are not used in 3/4; a whole bar rest is used instead.

iii) Although it is normally easier to see all the main beats if you write rests out in full (with each beat having a rest of its own where needed), you can use dotted rests in certain places (such as at the start of a bar in 4/4 time).

For example:

Both of these bars are acceptable.

This bar is *incorrect* because the rest starts midway through beat 1.

compound time signatures

<u>RULE 1</u>

Notes shorter than a dotted quarter note should be grouped together when they belong to one beat. This helps to clarify where the underlying dotted quarter note beat is.

For example, in 6/8 time the first three eighth notes (including any combination of eighth notes and sixteenth notes) should be beamed together. Similarly, the last three eighth notes should be beamed together.

This is correct

This bar is *incorrect* because although it contains the same order of notes as the example above, the notes are grouped as though in ¾ time.

<u>RULE 2</u>

The same rule for writing rests in simple time – that each beat must be completed with the appropriate rests – applies in compound time. When you write rests in compound time you must remember that each beat is equivalent to a dotted quarter note.

This is correct.

This is *incorrect* because it is written as though in ¾ time.

<u>Exception</u>

The whole note (semibreve) rest indicates a whole bar rest in all popular time signatures, including compound time signatures. Consequently, dotted half note rests are not used in ⅝ time as a whole bar rest is used instead.

There are specific additional rules about how the rests within each beat can be written. Remember, a beat in compound time lasts for a dotted quarter note.

- If the first two eighth notes of a beat are silent, a single quarter note rest should be used.

- If the last two eighth notes of a beat are silent, then two eighth note rests (rather than a single quarter note rest) should be used.

This is correct

This is *incorrect*

Distinguishing between ⅝ and ¾

As both ⅝ and ¾ time can contain six eighth notes, it is important to group them correctly. In ⅝ time there should always be a split between the 3rd and 4th eighth notes (because in ⅝ the beat is divided into two groups of three eighth notes).

Both lines of music below have the same note values, but notice how the grouping changes according to the time signature used.

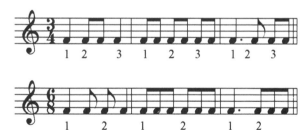

the exam

Below are some examples of the types of questions that candidates may be asked in this section of the exam. If you can't answer a question, then carefully re-read the preceding chapter and, if necessary, the preceding books in this series.

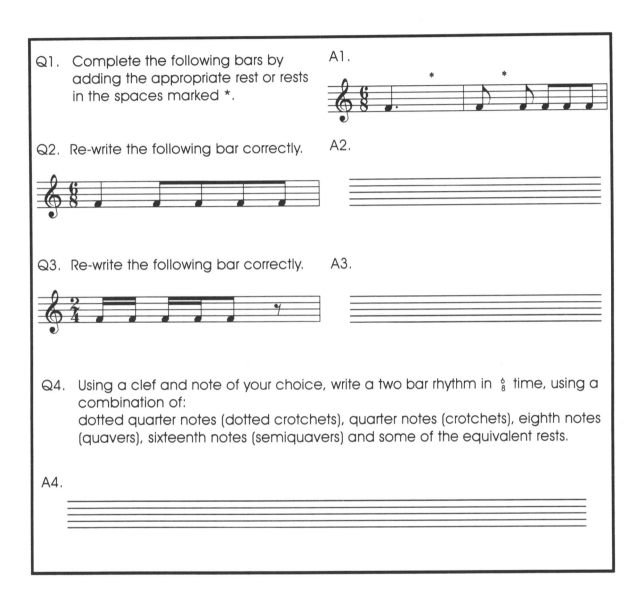

Q1. Complete the following bars by adding the appropriate rest or rests in the spaces marked *.

A1.

Q2. Re-write the following bar correctly.

A2.

Q3. Re-write the following bar correctly.

A3.

Q4. Using a clef and note of your choice, write a two bar rhythm in $\frac{6}{8}$ time, using a combination of:
dotted quarter notes (dotted crotchets), quarter notes (crotchets), eighth notes (quavers), sixteenth notes (semiquavers) and some of the equivalent rests.

A4.

Section Four – popular music

There are three areas of popular music that candidates will be asked questions on:

- influential groups, vocalists and instrumentalists
- commonly used instruments
- commonly used performance directions

influential performers

So that you increase your general knowledge of some of the performers and recording artists who have had the greatest influence on the development of popular music, at this grade you will be asked questions about the following:

- James Brown
- Eric Clapton
- Michael Jackson
- Nirvana

You may be asked to name:

- Some of their hit recordings.
- The instruments played by instrumentalists, and some of the bands they have played in.
- The period during which they performed or recorded.
- The styles of music with which they are associated.

Below is a short profile giving all the information you need to know about each artist and band for the Grade Three exam. We recommend, that as well as reading these profiles, you also listen to a range of recordings by the artists.

James Brown

American-born vocalist and songwriter, James Brown first had a top ten hit in the American R'n'B charts in 1956, with *Please, Please, Please*. Brown was a charismatic and energetic performer and achieved several more big R'n'B hits in the late 1950s and early 1960s, however it wasn't until 1965 that he became successful in the mainstream charts. *Papa's Got A Brand New Bag*, was the first of many successful recordings that he made during the late 1960s and early 1970s.

His innovative use of rhythms played a large part in the development of *funk* music. Brown was also influential in the development of *hip-hop* music, as his songs were some of the first to be 'sampled' and resulted in some of the biggest mainstream hits by a variety of hip-hop artists. Brown is widely recognised as one of popular music's most unique vocalists and performers. Although (at the time of writing) his last major chart success was during the 1980s, he continues to tour and has a devoted fan base world-wide.

These are some of his most famous recordings:

- *Prisoner Of Love*
- *Get Up (I feel like being a) Sex Machine*
- *Papa's Got A Brand New Bag*

- *I Got You (I Feel Good)*
- *Livin' In America*
- *Get Up Offa That Thing*

Eric Clapton

British-born guitarist, Eric Clapton first achieved notoriety with his blues-based guitar style whilst playing with bands such as *The Yardbirds* and *John Mayall's Bluesbreakers* during the early 1960s. In 1966, he teamed up with drummer Ginger Baker and bassist Jack Bruce to form the highly successful rock improvisation based trio, *Cream*, who stayed together for two years. During this period Clapton became widely regarded as one of the world's premier electric guitarists, and his style has inspired vast numbers of guitarists ever since.

Clapton went onto to play briefly with various other groups, such as *Blind Faith* and *Derek And The Dominos*. His solo album *461 Ocean Boulevard*, released in 1974, marked a distinct change of style to shorter commercial songs, with the emphasis more on Clapton's vocals rather than his guitar playing. During the 1990s he made some of his most commercially successful recordings ever, and (at the time of writing) Clapton is still performing sell-out concerts on a regular basis.

Some of his most famous recordings are:

- *Sunshine Of Your Love (recorded with Cream)*
- *Layla (originally recorded with Derek and the Dominos)*
- *Lay Down Sally*
- *I Shot The Sheriff*
- *Wonderful Tonight*
- *Tears in Heaven*

Michael Jackson

American-born, singer/songwriter, Michael Jackson first had success with four of his brothers in the group *The Jackson Five* on the Motown record label in 1970 (with each of their first four singles reaching number one in the USA). The following year, Michael Jackson released his debut solo single, *Got To Be There*, which was a hit both in the USA and the UK.

In 1979, working with the record producer Quincy Jones, Jackson released the solo album *Off The Wall* which sold 10 million copies world-wide. This established him as a hugely successful and influential solo artist.

His 1982 album *Thriller* became a number one album in the USA and the UK and produced several hit singles, such as *Billie Jean* and *Beat It*. The videos for both these singles likewise became hits due to the impressive choreography and special effects. Sales of the album have exceeded 60 million copies world-wide, making it one of the most commercially successful albums of all time.

Jackson has continued to have massive hits since then – although none have surpassed the success of *Thriller*. Throughout his career, whether as a solo artist, or with his brothers (the group was re-named *The Jacksons* when they moved from the Motown to the Epic label in 1975), Michael Jackson has produced highly danceable mainstream pop, and he has achieved his global popularity through the quality of his song-writing, singing and presentation skills.

Some of his most famous recordings are:

Jackson 5/The Jacksons:

- *I'll Be There*
- *ABC*
- *Blame It On The Boogie*

Michael Jackson (solo):

- *Got to Be There*
- *Don't Stop 'Till You Get Enough*
- *Billie Jean*
- *Beat It*
- *Thriller*

Nirvana

The American group Nirvana was formed in 1986 by Kurt Cobain and Chris Novoselic. The band had several different drummers, and initially another guitarist for the first recordings, but the line-up for the classic album *Nevermind*, released in 1991, was:

Kurt Cobain – vocals/guitar

Chris Novoselic – bass

Dave Grohl – drums

This album changed the rock scene forever, as for the first time a hard-hitting punk influence was fused with a more mainstream rock sound – the resulting fusion was known as 'grunge'. Mixing melodic and emotive vocal lines with a rebellious and angry sound, Nirvana gained an enormous youth following and the album sold in vast quantities.

Nirvana only recorded one further studio album, *In Utero* in 1993, before Cobain committed suicide in 1994. His early death was mourned by fans across the globe. Despite having such a short career, Nirvana's influence in the development of popular music is immense, and many bands still continue to emulate them.

Some of the group's most famous recordings are:

- About A Girl
- Smells Like Teen Spirit
- Lithium
- Come As You Are
- Polly
- Penny Royal Tea

Kurt Cobain – vocalist and guitarist with Nirvana

instruments

So that you have a basic knowledge of the instruments that are commonly used in popular music, you may be asked questions about the following instruments:

- electric and acoustic guitars
- bass guitars
- keyboards
- drum kit
- saxophones
- brass instruments

Below is a description of the instruments – giving all the information you need to know about each instrument for the Grade Three examination. We recommend that you try to hear each of the instruments being played – either live, or at least on a recording.

electric and acoustic guitars

- Standard electric and acoustic guitars are normally made of wood and have six steel strings. Nylon strung acoustic guitars also exist, but these are more widely used in classical than in popular music.

- The strings on a standard guitar are normally tuned to E, A, D, G, B and E, starting from the lowest string. There are two octaves between the two E strings. Different notes are produced through changing the length of a string by the player pressing on different places on the fingerboard of the guitar. The fingerboard is divided into halfsteps (semitones) by the use of metal frets.

- Although the strings can be picked with the fingers, normally in popular music a small plastic device known as a *plectrum* (or *pick*) is used to strike the strings. The strings can be played simultaneously to create chords or individually for single-note lead playing.

- On electric guitars the sound is produced by the vibration of the steel strings being electrically 'picked up' by an in-built device called a *pick up* and then amplified. On acoustic guitars the sound is also produced by the vibration of the strings, but with the hollow body of the guitar amplifying the sound.

- An electric guitar needs to be played through an *amplifier* and *speaker* in order to be heard. The term *amp* can refer to an amplifier and speaker contained in one unit, or a unit which contains only an amplifier. In the latter case, a separate unit containing a speaker is needed. This is often referred to as a *cab* (short for speaker cabinet). The distinctive sound of an electric guitar is created by the interaction of the guitar, amplifier and speaker.

- Although acoustic guitars can be played without amplification, they usually require it during performances in order to match the volume of other instruments. Acoustic guitars can be amplified by placing a microphone in front of the 'sound-hole' of the guitar, or by attaching a *pick up*.

bass guitars

- A standard bass guitar is usually made of wood and has a similar shape (but slightly larger size) to an electric guitar. The standard bass guitar has four strings that, starting from the lowest string, are tuned to E, A, D and G, an octave lower than standard guitar strings. Different notes are produced through changing the length of a string by the player pressing on different places on the fingerboard of the bass guitar. The fingerboard is normally divided into halfsteps (semitones) by the use of metal frets, although, some players use *fretless* basses to enable them to *slide* between notes more easily.

- In recent years, five string basses (which have an extra B string added below the E string) have become increasingly used in some forms of popular music. Occasionally, six string basses (where in addition to the B string, a C string is added above the G string) are also used by some players.

- Bass strings are normally picked with the fingers, although some players prefer to use a *plectrum*. Although some chords can be played on the bass guitar, most bass parts are single-note lines.

- The sound of a bass guitar is produced by the vibration of the steel strings being electrically 'picked up' by the instrument's in-built *pick up* and then amplified. Bass amplifiers and speakers have different specifications to guitar amplifiers, as they are built to reproduce the lower frequency range of the bass guitar.

keyboards

- Although pianos are the most traditional of all modern keyboard instruments, in contemporary popular music electric pianos, electronic keyboards and synthesisers are more commonly used. Collectively, these are known as *keyboards*.

- Keyboards are made in many different sizes, but the notes are always laid out like a piano, with the white keys producing the natural notes (C D E F G A B) and the black keys producing the flats and sharps.

- The keys on pianos and on good quality keyboards are *touch sensitive*. This means that the keys respond to how hard or softly the player touches them and enables the player to play with greater expression. Some electric keyboards also have *weighted* keys, to re-create the feel of a piano.

- Pianos have foot pedals attached that enable the player to either strengthen and sustain notes, or to soften and mute notes. Some keyboards also have similar pedals, particularly a sustain or volume pedal.

- Electronic keyboards usually have a variety of in-built piano and organ sounds, as well as a wide range of other *instrumental* sounds which re-create the sound of specific instruments. *Sampled* sounds (where real instruments have been digitally recorded) are usually more realistic than *synthesised* sounds, which are created electronically. Keyboards can also have many unique *synthesised* sounds, which do not emulate the sound of traditional instruments, and can be interesting musical sounds in their own right.

- The keys on many keyboards can be split into different sections and assigned to different sounds to allow the player to play, for example, a bass part and chords, or string and brass sounds.

- Many electronic keyboards have small in-built amplifiers and speakers, but for live performances they need to be amplified to achieve sufficient volume.

drum kit

- A drum kit consists of various percussion instruments arranged together so that they can all be played by one person using both hands and both feet.

- The drums shells themselves are made of wood, metal or synthetic materials, and are completed with *drum heads* (traditionally known as *skins*) made from plastic.

- Drums are usually played using wooden *drumsticks* (which sometimes have nylon tips). To achieve a different and quieter sound sometimes special *brushes* are used instead of sticks.

- The cymbals which complete the kit are made of metal – usually brass.

- A standard drum kit is made up of the following:

a) *bass* (or *kick*) *drum* which is struck with a foot-operated pedal

b) *snare drum*

c) one or more high *tom toms* and a low (*floor*) *tom tom*;

d) *ride cymbal*

e) *crash cymbal*

f) pair of cymbals known as a *hi hat* (which can be closed or opened with a foot operated pedal).

saxophones

- There are different sizes of saxophone but the two most commonly used in popular music are the *tenor saxophone* and the *alto saxophone*.
  Baritone saxophones are sometimes used as part of a *horn section* and *soprano saxophones* are sometimes used for lead solos.

- The body of the saxophone is hollow and made of brass. Air is blown through the body via the mouthpiece, where a *reed* (a small strip of cane) is attached. The reed vibrates producing sound waves which

then resonate through the body of the saxophone. Mouthpieces are made out of either ebonite (rubber) or metal, both of which have a different sound quality.

- In a concert setting, saxophones are usually amplified by using a microphone connected to a P.A. system.

brass instruments

- The most commonly used brass instruments in popular music are trumpets and trombones and both instruments are made of brass. There are different types of trumpets, but the most commonly used ones are called *B♭ trumpets*.

  There are different sizes of trombone, but the most commonly used ones are the *tenor trombone* and the *bass trombone*. The tenor trombone is higher in pitch, and is more often used in popular music, than the bass trombone.

- The sound is produced in both instruments by air blown through the instrument: the player's lips vibrate and create sound waves which are amplified by the body of the instrument. Different notes are produced by changing the amount of tension in the lips.

- Trumpets also have three *valves*, each of which when pressed changes the length of the tube and produces further notes. In trombones the length of the tube is changed, and further notes produced, by the use of a *slide*. There are also, lesser used, *valve trombones*, which operate in a similar way as trumpets.

- In a concert setting, brass instruments are sometimes amplified using microphones and a P.A. system.

musical signs and terminology

So that you have a basic knowledge of the common musical signs and terminology used in popular music you will be asked questions on the following areas:

- tempo
- dynamics
- articulation
- directions for rests and repeats

So that the signs and terminology learnt in theory can be effectively used in a practical way, you should be able to:

- understand the practical differences in tempo between different bpm (metronome) markings
- explain in practical terms the meaning of different dynamic markings
- add dynamic markings to a chord progression or melody
- add articulation markings to a chord progression or melody
- understand and use directions for rests, repeated bars and repeat marks

tempo

In popular music the most commonly used indication of tempo is to specify the *beats per minute* (*bpm*) – this can also be referred to as the *metronome marking*.

♩ = 60

This means that there are 60 quarter note beats per minute.

♩ = 120

This means that there are 120 quarter note beats per minute. So a tempo of ♩ = 120 bpm is twice as fast as a tempo of ♩ = 60 bpm.

dynamics

Below are the symbols used to indicate how quietly or loudly notes or phrases should be played. The symbols are based on abbreviations of Italian terms:

symbol	meaning	Italian term
pp	very softly	pianissimo
p	softly	piano
mp	moderately softly	mezzo piano
mf	moderately strongly	mezzo forte
f	strongly	forte
ff	very strongly	fortissimo

You can add more *p*s or *f*s (normally to a maximum of three) to instruct the performer to play extremely softly or extremely strongly.

articulation

The following symbols tell the performer how to play specific notes.

A dot above or below the notehead means 'play the note short' – about half its normal length. This is known as a *staccato* dot.

A straight line above or below the notehead means 'play the note to its full length and *lean* on it slightly'. This is known as a *tenuto* mark.

A 'V' lying on its side above or below a notehead means 'accent the note'. This is known as an *accent*.

Slurs are used where notes should be played together as smoothly as possible. For example, saxophonists and brass instrumentalists will play all the slurred notes in one breath, without accenting any of them. Guitarists and bass players slur notes by 'hammering-on' or 'pulling-off' onto the notes with their fretting fingers, instead of picking the string again as normal for each new note.

directions for rests

A bar of rest is indicated by a whole (semibreve) rest. If there is more than one bar of rest, a horizontal line is written through the bar with the number of silent bars written above it.

This is much easier for a performer to count than eight separate bars containing whole rests.

directions for repeats

If one bar is to be repeated then the symbol ⁄. can be used. This symbol can be repeated as necessary.

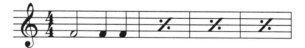

To indicate that a section of music should be repeated (played twice) *repeat marks* are used. A double bar line, followed by two dots either side of the middle line of the staff, indicates the start of the section to be repeated. Two dots either side of the middle line of the staff, followed by a double bar line, indicate the end of the section. If there are no initial repeat dots then repeat from the beginning of the piece.

Repeat marks can also be used for chord charts, and any number of bars may be included within the repeat marks.

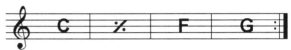

If the section is to be repeated more than once, the number of times it is to be played is written above the last repeat dots.

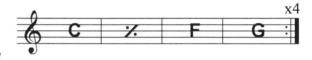

This means play the phrase four times in total.

the exam

Below are some examples of the types of questions that candidates may be asked in this section of the exam. If you can't answer a question, then carefully re-read the preceding chapter.

Q1. Name two types of music that James Brown has influenced.

A1. _____

Q2. What type of music did the band *Cream* play?

A2. _____

Q3. Name four hit recordings by Michael Jackson, including and identifying at least one recorded with The Jackson 5 / The Jacksons.

A3. _____

   _____

Q4. Name the open strings on a standard four string bass guitar from low to high.

A4. _____

Q5. Name 4 parts of a drum kit.

A5. _____

Q6. How should a phrase be played if it has the performance direction pp ?

A6. _____

Q7. Using chord symbols, write a chord chart for the following chord progression: 2 bars of Am7, 2 bars of Cmaj7, 2 bars of Am7, 2 bars of Cmaj7.
   Use repeat markings, i.e. repeat bar signs and repeat section dots.

A7. _____

Section Five – harmony

In this section of the exam you will be asked to demonstrate your knowledge of:

■ Triads built from the C, G, D, F and B♭ major scales and the A, E, B, D, and G natural minor scales.

■ The technical names for the chords built on the 1st, 4th and 5th degrees of the major scale.

■ The tonic, subdominant and dominant chords in the major keys listed above.

■ V – I (perfect) and IV – I (plagal) cadences in the major keys listed above.

■ The application of major and natural minor scales, listed above, in improvisation.

So that the harmony learnt in theory can be used effectively in a practical way, you should be able to do the following:

■ Write out, and identify, the triads built from the scales of C, G, D, F and B♭ major, and A, E, B, D, and G natural minor.

■ Write out, and identify, the I (tonic), IV (subdominant) and V (dominant) triads and the V7 (dominant) chords in major keys up to two sharps and two flats.

■ Identify and construct, chord progressions in the keys of C, G and F major, using V – I (perfect) and IV – I (plagal) cadences.

■ Identify which major or natural minor scale would be the most suitable to use for improvising over a given chord progression.

■ Write chord progressions over which the C, G or F major scales could be used for improvising.

the theory

The type of triad that can be built, by using three alternate notes, from each degree of a major scale is always the same for each particular scale degree, regardless of the key.

All major keys have the following pattern of triads:

I	II	III	IV	V	VI	VII
major	minor	minor	major	major	minor	diminished

Below are the triads that occur in the keys of C, G, D, F and B♭ major.

Degree:	I	II	III	IV	V	VI	VII
C major:	C	Dm	Em	F	G	Am	B°
G major:	G	Am	Bm	C	D	Em	F#°
D major:	D	Em	F#m	G	A	Bm	C#°
F major:	F	Gm	Am	B♭	C	Dm	E°
B♭ major:	B♭	Cm	Dm	E♭	F	Gm	A°

Notice that the triads built on the 1st, 4th and 5th degrees are major, the triads built on the 2nd, 3rd and 6th degrees are minor, and the triad built on the 7th degree is diminished.

The type of triad that can be built, by taking three alternate notes, from each degree of a natural minor scale is always the same for each particular scale degree, regardless of the key.

All natural minor keys have the following pattern of triads:

I	II	III	IV	V	VI	VII
major	diminished	major	minor	minor	major	major

Below are the triads built from the scales of A, E, B, D and G natural minor.

Degree:	I	II	III	IV	V	VI	VII
A minor:	Am	B°	C	Dm	Em	F	G
E minor:	Em	F#°	G	Am	Bm	C	D
B minor:	Bm	C#°	D	Em	F#m	G	A
D minor:	Dm	E°	F	Gm	Am	B♭	C
G minor:	Gm	A°	B♭	Cm	Dm	E♭	F

Notice that the triads built on the 1st, 4th and 5th degrees are minor, the triads built on the 3rd, 6th and 7th degrees are major and the triad built on the 2nd degree is diminished.

Degrees of the scale and the chords that are built on them, are traditionally, and still widely, identified using Roman numerals. This system provides a useful shortcut for writing chords, as it identifies the 'type' of triad as well as the 'position' of the triad in the scale. Below are the triads from the C major and A natural minor scales identified using the Roman numeral system. By using the formulae below you can work out which triads can be built from any major or natural minor scale.

C major	Triad:	C	Dm	Em	F	G	Am	B°
	Roman numerals:	I	IIm	IIIm	IV	V	VIm	VII°

A natural minor	Triad:	Am	B°	C	Dm	Em	F	G
	Roman numerals:	Im	II°	♭III	IVm	Vm	♭VI	♭VII

There follows a brief explanation as to why the triads from the natural minor scale are numbered in this way. In the examination, however, you will only be asked to identify, or write out the pattern of triads.

Supplementary explanation

The triads built from the natural minor scale are numbered in comparison to the triads built from the major scale with the same keynote. The flat sign before the chords built on the 3rd, 6th and 7th degrees indicates that the roots of these chords are one half step (semitone) lower than the roots of the corresponding chords built from the major scale with the same keynote.

For example, in the key of D major the 3rd, 6th and 7th notes are F#, B and C#. In the scale of D natural minor the 3rd, 6th and 7th notes are F, B♭ and C. Therefore the roots of the triads built on these degrees of the D natural minor scale are all a half step lower than the roots of the triads built on the same degrees of the D major scale.

Some musicians (particularly in the USA) prefer to use standard numbers in place of Roman numerals – this method of identifying chords is called the 'Nashville Numbering System'.

In this book we use the Roman numeral system. In the exam, answers can be expressed using either system providing you are consistent in your usage.

C major	Triad:	C	Dm	Em	F	G	Am	B°
	Nashville numbering:	1	2m	3m	4	5	6m	7°

Some musicians prefer to use a dash (-) in place of the 'm' in minor chord symbols when using Nashville Numbering.

The Nashville Numbering system is designed to be used primarily with major keys. Its approach to minor keys is pragmatic: the way the chords are identified in minor keys depends upon the structure of the chord progression and the preferences of the arranger. For example, the tonic chord in a minor key might be written as either '1m' (i.e. first chord of the key and minor) or as '6m' (stemming from its position in the relative major key).

A natural minor	Triad:	Am	B°	C	Dm	Em	F	G
	Nashville numbering: (tonic minor key version)	1m	2°	b3	4m	5m	b6	b7
	Nashville numbering: (relative major key version)	6m	7°	1	2m	3m	4	5

In the first version, the chords are numbered according to their relationship to the major key with the same keynote (i.e. A major, in this example). In the second version, the minor key tonality is ignored and the chords are numbered purely according to their position in the relative major key (i.e. C major, in this example). Whichever version of Nashville Numbering is used for minor keys, it is essential that it is identified at the outset. This can be done by adding above the chord progression either 'Written with minor key numbering' or 'Written with relative major key numbering'.

technical names

Chords that occur on each degree of the scale have names that originate in classical music terminology. The chord that occurs on the first degree of the scale is known as the *tonic*. The chord that occurs on the fourth degree is known as the *subdominant*. The chord that occurs on the fifth degree is known as the *dominant*. The dominant chord is often played as a four note *dominant seventh* chord.

Below are the tonic, subdominant and dominant seventh chords in the keys of C, G, D, F and Bb major.

technical name / key	C major	G major	D major	F major	Bb major
tonic	C	G	D	F	Bb
subdominant	F	C	G	Bb	Eb
dominant	G7	D7	A7	C7	F7

cadences

Cadences are musical 'punctuation marks' created by using a combination of chords that imply a resting place. A minimum of two chords have to be used in order to create the *resolution*. Cadences nearly always appear at the end of songs, however they also occur in other places during the course of a song, such as at the end of a phrase or verse.

Historically, two cadences that have been used extensively both in classical and popular music are the *V – I cadence* (also called the *perfect cadence*) and the *IV – I cadence* (also called the *plagal cadence*).

The *V – I cadence* is the cadence which creates the strongest and most complete ending to a phrase. In the key of C major this can be played as either G to C, or G7 to C. By playing the V chord as a dominant 7th chord (rather than just a major triad) a stronger sounding cadence is created. Consequently, V – I cadences are often played as V7 – I.

The *IV – I cadence* is another cadence which is often used to end a musical phrase, although it is more subtle than the V – I cadence. In the key of C major this is played as F to C.

constructing chord progressions

At this grade you will be asked to write chord progressions only in the keys of C, G and F major. There are many different approaches to writing chord progressions, but deciding how effective the chords sound in any particular combination is the most important consideration. Here are a few tips on writing chord progressions that will help you get started.

- So that you can choose from the full range of chords, you need to know all the triads that are in the key. It is also useful to know which dominant 7th chord occurs in each key

- Starting the chord progression with the *tonic chord* will help to instantly define the pitch and nature of the key.

- Using a V – I or IV – I cadence at the end of the progression will help to create a sense of 'reaching a resting point' or a feeling of 'arriving home'.

This progression, in the key of G major, starts with the tonic chord and ends with a V – I cadence.

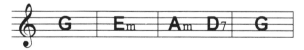

improvisation

Major scales are used for improvising in major keys. For example, if a chord progression uses chords from the key of C major, then the C major scale would be an appropriate scale to use for improvising.

Natural minor scales are used for improvising in minor keys. For example, if a chord progression uses chords built from the A natural minor scale, then the A natural minor scale would be an appropriate scale to use for improvising.

Identifying which key the chords in a progression belong to will help you decide which scale to use for improvisation. Because the chords from any major scale and its relative natural minor are the same, it is important to look at how the chord progression is structured in order to correctly identify the key. Normally, a chord progression will start and finish on the I (tonic) chord, and this will indicate whether the progression is in the major or relative minor key.

For example, in the following two chord progressions, although all the chords that are featured can occur in the keys of both C major and A minor, the first progression is in C major and the second one is in A minor.

The C major scale would be a good choice for improvisation over this progression.

The A natural minor scale would be a good choice for improvisation over this progression.

When you are writing a chord progression to be used as a backing for improvisation the same process as described above applies. Firstly, work out the possible chords that can built from each degree of the scale to be used, and then experiment with different possible combinations until you come up with a progression that you like. Remember that using a V-I or IV-I cadence is a straightforward and effective way to create an ending to a progression.

Below are some examples of the types of questions that candidates may be asked in this section of the exam. If you can't answer a question, then carefully re-read the preceding chapter.

Q1. Using chord symbols, write out the major, minor and diminished triads that can be built from the E natural minor scale.

A1. _____

Q2. Using chord symbols, name the tonic, subdominant and dominant triads built from the F major scale.

A2. Tonic: _____ Subdominant: _____ Dominant: _____

Q3. What type of cadence is formed between the chords in bars 3 and 4?

| B♭ | E♭ | F7 | B♭ |

A3. _____

Q4. Using the chord symbols of at least three different chords, write a four bar chord progression in the key of G major with the last two bars forming a IV-I (plagal) cadence.

A4.

Q5. Name a suitable scale that could be used for improvising over the following chord progression.

| B♭ | Cm | F7 | B♭ |

A5. _____

Q6. Using the chord symbols of at least three different chords, write a four bar chord progression over which the F major scale could be used for improvisation.

A6.

Section Six – transposition

In this section of the exam you will be asked to demonstrate your ability to transpose chord progressions. In particular, you will be asked to transpose a chord progression either up or down a whole step (whole tone) within a range of keys up to two sharps and two flats.

the theory

To *transpose* a chord progression means to re-write it changing the key that it is written in. The 'quality' of the chords (major, minor, dominant) stays exactly the same, as does their relationship to each other and to the key centre – only the overall pitch changes.

Transposition is a useful skill to have because it means that you do not always have to play songs in their original keys. For example, if you are accompanying a singer who finds that the melody of a song is too low you can change the key to suit the range of the singer's voice. You might also want to change the key of a song to make it more suitable to play on your instrument. For example, the keys that suit keyboards are not always the keys that suit guitars.

There are two different methods that you can use to transpose chord progressions. Both methods will give exactly the same result.

chord numbers

Identify the key of the original chord progression and work out the chord numbers for each of the chords. Using the chord numbers then work out the chords in the new key.

For example, to transpose the following chord progression into the key of B♭ major, the first step is to identify the key of the progression.

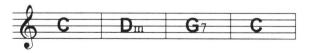

The preceding chord progression is in the key of C major because:

- the progression starts and ends on a C major triad.

- all the chords are in the key of C major.

- the movement of G7 to C forms a V-I (perfect cadence) in the key of C major.

Having worked out the key of the progression, next identify the key chord – which will have the chord number 'I'. From this, the other chord numbers can then be worked out. You can check that you have worked them out correctly by ensuring that the chord type for each degree corresponds to the standard major scale pattern of triads and dominant 7th chords.

The chord numbers for the above progression are:

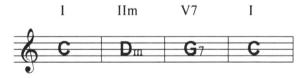

To transpose the chord progression to B♭ major, you need to work out what the I, IIm, and V7 chords are in the key of B♭ major. To do this, count up the degrees of the B♭ major scale to find the root of each chord. (The 2nd of B♭ is C, the 5th of B♭ is F). Remember, the chord quality for each chord remains the same as in the original key, therefore the chord progression transposed into the key of B♭ major will be:

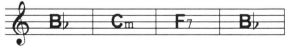

intervals

Another way to transpose the chord progression is to change the root note of each chord by the interval requested. For the Grade Three exam, this will be either up or down one whole step (whole tone). You work this out by first identifying what the original key is, and then deciding if the key you have to transpose the progression into is a whole step above or below the original key.

Taking the same example as before – transposing from C major into B♭ major:

B♭ is one whole step below C, so for this transposition the root note of each chord needs to be moved down one whole step. As in the previous method, the chord types stay the same as in the original key.

- The C chord would move down a whole step to become a B♭ chord.

- The Dm chord would move down a whole step to become a Cm chord.

- The G7 chord would move down a whole step to become an F7 chord.

Tip

With both methods it is essential that you take account of any sharps or flats that occur in the new key so that the correct enharmonic spelling is used. For example, in the key of F major the IV chord should always be named B♭, rather than A#.

the exam

Below are some examples of the types of questions that candidates may be asked in this section of the exam. If you can't answer a question then carefully re-read the preceding chapter.

Once you've worked through the questions you can check your answers by looking in the back of the book.

Q1. Transpose the following chord progression into the key of D major.

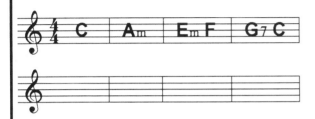

Q2. Transpose the following chord progression into the key of D minor.

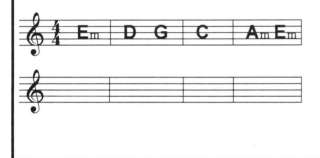

Section Seven – sample answers

Note that all the answers below are 'sample answers' and for several questions there are a range of other answers that would also be acceptable.

Section One – scales and keys   *[Max. 20 marks]*

A1.   D   F   G   A♭   A   C   D

A2.   G   A   B♭   C   D   E♭   F   G

A3.   1   ♭3   4   ♭5   5   ♭7   8

A4.

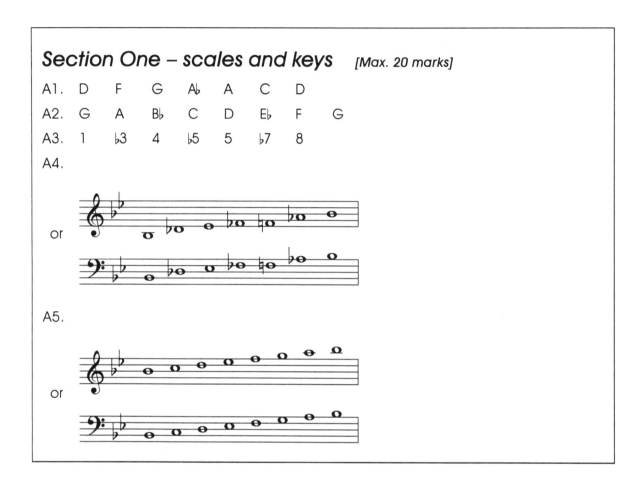

A5.

Section Two – chords   *[Max. 20 marks]*

A1.   F A C E♭

A2.   minor 7th chord

A3.   1 3 5 7

A4.   flattened (or diminished) fifth

A5.

Section Three – rhythm notation [Max. 10 marks]

A1.

A2.

A3.

A4.

Section Four – knowledge of popular music [Max. 15 marks]

A1. Funk and hip-hop

A2. Improvised rock music.

A3. Thriller, Beat It, Got To Be There, (plus with The Jacksons) Blame It On The Boogie.

A4. E A D and G.

A5. snare, bass (kick) drum, hi hat, tom tom (ride or crash cymbal would also be acceptable).

A6. Very softly.

A7.

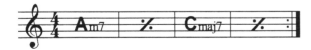

Section Five – harmony   [Max. 25 marks]

A1.   Em   F#°   G   Am   Bm   C   D

A2.   Tonic: F. Subdominant: B♭. Dominant: C.

A3.   V7 – I ('Perfect cadence', or '5⁷ to 1' would also be acceptable)

A4.

| G | B~m~ | C | G |

A5.   B♭ major

A6.

| F | A~m~ | D~m~ C~7~ | F |

Section Six – transposition   [Max. 10 marks]

A1.

| $\frac{4}{4}$ D | B~m~ | F♯~m~ G | A~7~ D |

A2.

| $\frac{4}{4}$ D~m~ | C F | B♭ | G~m~ D~m~ |

Examination Entry Form for LCM
Popular Music Theory examination.

GRADE THREE

PLEASE COMPLETE CLEARLY USING BLOCK CAPITAL LETTERS

SESSION (Summer/Winter): _____ YEAR: _____

Preferred Examination Centre (if known): _____
If left blank, you will be examined at the nearest examination centre to your home address.

Candidate Details:

Candidate Name (as to appear on certificate):

_____

Address: _____

_____

_____ Postcode: _____

Tel. No. (day): _____ (evening): _____

Teacher Details:

Teacher Name (as to appear on certificate): _____

Registry Tutor Code (if applicable): _____

Address: _____

_____ Postcode: _____

Tel. No. (day): _____ (evening): _____

The standard LCM entry form is NOT valid for Popular Music Theory entries. Entry to the examination is only possible via this original form.

Photocopies of this form will not be accepted under *any* circumstances.

IMPORTANT NOTES

- It is the candidate's responsibility to have knowledge of, and comply with, the current syllabus requirements. Where candidates are entered for examinations by teachers, the teacher must take responsibility that candidates are entered in accordance with the current syllabus requirements. In particular, from 2005 it is important to check that the contents of this book match the syllabus that is valid at the time of entry.

- For candidates with special needs, a letter giving details should be attached.

- Theory dates are the same worldwide and are fixed annually by LCM. Details of entry deadlines and examination dates are obtainable from the Examinations Registry.

- Submission of this entry is an undertaking to abide by the current regulations as listed in the current syllabus and any subsequent regulations updates published by the LCM / Examinations Registry.

- UK entries should be sent to The Examinations Registry, Registry House, Churchill Mews, Dennett Rd, Croydon, Surrey CR0 3JH

- Overseas entrants should contact the LCM / Examinations Registry for details of their international representatives.

Examination Fee   £ _____

Late Entry Fee (if applicable)   £ _____

Total amount submitted: £ _____

Cheques or postal orders should be made payable to The Examinations Registry.
Entries cannot be made by credit card.

A current list of fees is available from the Examinations Registry.

The Examinations Registry
Registry House
Churchill Mews
Dennett Road
Croydon
Surrey, U.K.
CR0 3JH

Tel: 020 8665 7666
Fax: 020 8665 7667
Email: ExamRegistry@aol.com